PORCH, LAWN AND COTTAGE FURNITURE

TWO COMPLETE CATALOGS,
ca. 1904 and 1926

Rustic Hickory Furniture Co.

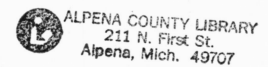

York

Copyright © 1991 by Dover Publications, Inc.
All rights reserved under Pan American and International Copyright Conventions.

Published in Canada by General Publishing Company, Ltd., 30 Lesmill Road, Don Mills, Toronto, Ontario.
Published in the United Kingdom by Constable and Company, Ltd., 3 The Lanchesters, 162–164 Fulham Palace Road, London W6 9ER.

This Dover edition, first published in 1991, is an unabridged republication of the catalogs titled *Rustic Hickory Furniture Co.,* ca. 1904, and *Rustic Hickory: A Reflection of Nature's Beauty,* 1926. The Introduction by Victor M. Linoff was specially written for this edition.

Manufactured in the United States of America
Dover Publications, Inc., 31 East 2nd Street, Mineola, N.Y. 11501

Library of Congress Cataloging-in-Publication Data

Rustic Hickory Furniture Co.
    Porch, lawn and cottage furniture : two complete catalogs, ca. 1904 and 1926 / Rustic Hickory Furniture Co.; edited by Victor M. Linoff. — Dover ed.
        p.   cm.
    Unabridged republication of the catalogs entitled: Rustic Hickory Furniture Co., ca. 1904 and Rustic hickory, 1926.
    ISBN 0-486-26531-5 (pbk.)
    1. Rustic Hickory Furniture Co.—Catalogs. 2. Country furniture—United States—History—20th century—Catalogs. I. Linoff, Victor M. II. Rustic Hickory Furniture Co. III. Rustic Hickory Furniture Co. Rustic hickory. IV. Title.
NK2439.R87A4 1991
684.1'029'0477291—dc20   90-45633
                                                              CIP

INTRODUCTION

THE HAUNTING VOICE of the wind singing in the tall pines . . . the gentle padding of feet on fallen leaves, exploring pathways along the forest's floor . . . afternoons of culture and enlightenment at summer chautauquas . . . the contemplation of magnificent sunsets from a rough-hewn chair on a cabin porch . . . pondering the cosmos after dark under heavens that sparkle like a jeweled wonder. These were idyllic Victorian notions of the great outdoors, evocative images that we are once again learning to cherish in this age of ever-increasing population, pollution and stress.

As the nineteenth century evolved, America's love affair with bucolic, pastoral settings was demonstrated time and again in many ways, not the least of which was in its growing desire for "rustic" furnishings. What better way to epitomize nature than through an emulation of it in everyday furniture?

"Vernacular" is a word historians have come to use for architectural and decorative art forms that represent the simplest, most common, most functional of designs—reflecting, to paraphrase Russell Lynes in *The Tastemakers,* a "highbrow appreciation of things lowbrow." Rustic furniture in its oldest sense was truly vernacular and unsophisticated; we generally use the term today, however, for "highbrow" interpretations of a closeness to nature.

Sylvan style had its modern origins in the gardens of eighteenth-century England, where its roots ran deep. In a cultural rebellion against the structured and formalized French society of Louis XIV, the English began designing gardens that were more natural in form. Eschewing the orderly composition of the European garden, the English garden gave the appearance of having always been there. Streams meandered, trees grew freely and footpaths took irregular courses.

Special furnishings were created to adorn these new-style gardens. Like the gardens themselves, garden furniture was designed to complement and imitate nature as closely as possible. Rustic style flourished throughout the eighteenth century. Even classical furniture designers like Thomas Chippendale offered rustic designs in their stylebooks.

As popular as the style became in England, it would take nearly a century for a "back to nature" philosophy to catch on in the United States and for what had been essentially outdoor furniture to move indoors. In the eighteenth century, America was struggling for its own identity. The revolution against English rule was also a rebellion against English fashion, design and style. And with the hardships of establishing a foothold in this new land and an economic base for a newly evolving society, most Americans were looking more toward luxury and comfort than toward the simple life they had been compelled to lead during the early years of the country's development.

By the mid-nineteenth century, the Industrial Revolution had emphatically shown that it would forever change the social and economic dynamics of the United States. A rural, agrarian population was rapidly becoming urbanized; cities were growing at an alarming rate. Attendant to increasing population, the pollution of industry was befouling the city, crime was increasing and disease was becoming more prevalent. When they could afford to, people escaped to the country, where the air was fresher and pastoral surroundings provided the opportunity to recharge body and mind.

One of the first and certainly most successful promoters of the healthful aspects of an exurban retreat was also, appropriately, the first prominent landscape gardener in the United States. Through four books and numerous articles, Andrew Jackson Downing (1815–1852), during his short life, had a profound influence on American taste and style. Although he recognized that the city was necessary to the growth of the nation, Downing espoused the country as the more beneficial to the human spirit. In *The*

Architecture of Country Houses (New York: Dover, 1969), first published in 1850, Downing explains his philosophy:

> It is the solitude and freedom of the family home in the country which constantly preserves the purity of the nation, and invigorates its intellectual powers. The battle of life, carried on in cities, gives a sharper edge to the weapon of character, but its temper is, for the most part, fixed amid those communings with nature and the family, where individuality takes its most natural and strongest development. (Preface, p. xix of Dover edition).
>
> . . . It is [within the country home] that the social virtues are more honestly practised, that the duties and graces of life have more meaning, that the character has more room to develop its best and finest traits than within the walls of cities.
>
> . . . The occupations of the country are full of health for both soul and body, and for the most refined as well as the most rustic taste. The heart has there, always within its reach, something on which to bestow its affections. . . . Every winding path throughout the woods, every secluded resting-place in the valley, every dell where the brook lives and sings, becomes part of our affections, friendship, joy, and sorrows. Happy is he who lives this life of a cultivated mind in the country! (p. 258)

Downing suggests that

> . . . a country house . . . should always be furnished with more chasteness and simplicity than a town house; because, it is in the country, if anywhere, that we should find essential ease and convenience always preferred to that love of effect and desire to dazzle, which is begotten, for the most part, by rivalry of mere wealth in town life. . . .
>
> The great desideratum in the furniture of country houses is, that it should be essentially *country-like*—which, we think, is attained only when it unites taste, comfort, and durability in the greatest degree. (pp. 409–10)

With regard to outdoor furnishings, Downing elsewhere offers the thought that "rustic seats, . . . placed here and there in the most inviting spots, will both heighten the charm and enable us to enjoy at leisure the quiet beauty around" (*Victorian Cottage Residences* [New York: Dover, 1981], p. 119). His introduction of rustic furnishings to this country started a fad, but a fad that would continue for nearly three-quarters of a century.

By the 1870s urban Americans were flocking to the country in droves. Those of sufficient means built summer "cottages," some of them quite splendid. Others vacationed in mountain retreats, of which the Adirondacks in upstate New York, with their natural beauty and their accessibility to the residents of New York City, was the first and largest. Large, rough-hewn wood lodges and cabins were built to accommodate the ever-increasing number of vacationers. The rugged outdoors was brought inside in the form of exposed log beams, stone fireplaces and furniture that "imitated" nature. This often deceptively simple furniture was generally handmade by skilled carpenters and artisans. So distinctive was the style that rustic furnishings of that locale are known as "Adirondack."

Through numerous books and articles, the entire nation seemed to rediscover the joys of rustic life. With Teddy Roosevelt's ascension to the Presidency in 1901, Americans were continually entertained by his outdoor exploits and adventures. A national clamoring for rustic style began to be heard, and factories started producing this furniture in sturdy, well-built designs.

Hickory was a popular wood for mass production because of its suppleness and pliability; young saplings could be easily bent into gentle curves around metal forms. With large, abundant stands of hickory readily available, Indiana became the leader in commercial production of rustic furniture at the turn of the century. One of the earliest Indiana factories was the Old Hickory Furniture Company of Martinsville, which began operation in 1890. Claiming to be "The Original Old Hickory Furniture Manufacturers," the company grew to be the largest in the nation, and was still producing rustic furniture into the Depression.

Close in size and output was the Rustic Hickory Furniture Company of La Porte, just a dozen miles from the shores of Lake Michigan in northwest Indiana. The company was established in 1902 to produce "furniture for the Porch, Lawn or Den."

The cover of the first catalog reprinted here, originally published around 1904, shows the imprint of Mandel Brothers, a large Chicago retailer established in 1855, and thus a major distributor for the Rustic Hickory line. With the exception of a dozen tables, the 94 pieces offered in the catalog are entirely seating furniture, from children's chairs to porch swings. By contrast, two decades later the Rustic Hickory catalog was offering 146 designs, which included bedroom furniture and a large number of outdoor pieces, including a tree seat, fencing and an octagonal summerhouse.

The twenty-year interval between the two catalogs provides an opportunity to observe how the mass-produced rustic style evolved from the height of its popularity to its waning years. Surprisingly, although one can perceive a slight simplification in the 1926 pieces (fewer spindles, more woven hickory), the overall design is remarkably similar, attesting to the enduring popularity of Rustic Hickory's prototypes. (Though no prices are printed in the second catalog, the 1927 price list, reproduced on pp. 71–73, is keyed to it.)

By the Depression, Americans had become concerned with new problems. Most of their energies were directed toward surviving that bleak period. There was little time to enjoy the benefits of the great outdoors. The rustic style's time had passed. Until its rediscovery in the mid-1970s, rustic furniture languished in disrepair on countless porches across this land, or was stowed away in barns, basements or attics. A few second-hand stores offered pieces at bargain prices.

These simple tributes to nature are now once more recognized for their creative form and execution and are considered fashionable for even the city home. The history of the rustic style has been the theme of a number of museum exhibitions, and examples are now part of permanent collections.

Let these two scarce catalogs be your window to another era, when life had a different meaning. As you peruse the pages, imagine yourself in a quaint and comfortable chair rocking away at sunset deep in the mountains, breathing in the cool, fresh air of evening, and you'll soon discover why this delightful furniture captured the fancy and hearts of Americans.

Victor M. Linoff

RUSTIC HICKORY

FOR PORCHES AND LAWNS

¶N all mankind there is a certain long-
ing for nature, a desire to be free from
the bondage of the artificial, and come
back to the real natural beauty found only
in nature itself.

¶ What furniture for the Porch, Lawn or Den could give
more genuine rest, comfort and pleasure, and appeal to one
more than Rustic Hickory, which being built of the strongest
of our native woods, with nature expressed in every design, is
in perfect harmony with the surroundings of the porch
and lawn?

¶ The frames are built of carefully selected hickory saplings
with the bark left on, sanded smooth to the white, and taking
on a beautiful polish with usage. The seats and backs are
woven by hand with smooth strips of the inner hickory
bark making them pliable, strong and comfortable.

¶ We aim to maintain a standard of strictly high grade
goods, making the test of quality of supreme importance.

¶ We have the facilities, the ability and the desire to excel in
our line of work; and we trust that a careful perusal of this
catalogue will convince you of our ability to execute anything in the line of Rustic Hickory Furniture.

¶ No order is too large, neither is it too small, for us to handle.

¶ Keep this catalogue for reference; you will have frequent
occasion to consult it. Yours very truly,

Rustic Hickory Furniture Company

LA PORTE, INDIANA, U. S. A.

SUGGESTIVE OF EASE AND COMFORT

Kindergarten Chairs for the Children.

BEGIN
YOUR ORDER
WITH
THESE

No. 6—CHILD'S CHAIR. Price $1.20.   No. 7—CHILD'S ROCKER. Price $1.60.

Spindle backs.
Seats 12 inches wide, 10 inches deep, 11 inches high.
Weight, per dozen, 60 pounds.

No. 8—CHILD'S CHAIR. Price $1.50.   No. 9—CHILD'S ROCKER. Price $1.90.

Woven seats and backs.
Seats 12 inches wide, 10 inches deep, and 11 inches high.
They Sell at Sight.

The Weights Given Herein Are Approximately Correct.

No. 10—CHILD'S CHAIR.
Price $1.50.

No. 11—CHILD'S ROCKER.
Price $2.00.

Extreme height, 23 inches.
Seats 13 inches wide, 11 inches deep, 11 inches high.
Weight, 8 pounds each.

Simplicity and Strength Are the Essential Points In a Child's Chair.

No. 12—CHILD'S CHAIR.
Price $2.00.

No. 13—CHILD'S ROCKER.
Price $2.50.

Double woven seats and backs.
Extreme height, 24 inches.
Seats 12 inches wide, 10 inches deep, 11 inches high.
Weight, 8 pounds each.

Look For the Green Label—The Genuine Only, Bears Our Trade Mark.

No. 16—CHAIR.   Price $2.00.   No. 17—ROCKER.   Price $2.50.

Extreme height, 40 inches.   Seats 18 inches wide, 16 inches deep.
Weight, 20 pounds each.

A Cheap Chair That Will Stand All Manner of Abuse.

No. 18—CHAIR.   Price $2.25.   No. 19—ROCKER.   Price $2.75.

Extreme height, 38 inches.   Seats 17 inches wide, 15 inches deep.
Weight, 15 pounds each.

A Light Arm Chair of Unusual Strength and Grace.

4

No. 22—CHAIR. Price $2.75.   No. 23—ROCKER. Price $3.25.

Extreme height, 36 inches. Seats 17 inches wide, 15 inches deep.

Weight, 15 pounds each.

Very Popular.

Not Affected by Rain, Sunshine, or Any Kind of Weather.

VERANDA OF THE COUNTRY CLUB, LINCOLN, NEBRASKA

Every Joint Nailed and Glued. Every Rocker Bolted On.

No. 20—CHAIR.   Price $2.75.   No. 21—ROCKER.   Price $3.25.

Straight arm.   (Larger than Nos. 18 and 19.)
Extreme height, 40 inches.   Seats 18 inches wide and 16 inches deep.
Weight, 20 pounds each.

Strong, Serviceable and Attractive.

No. 24—CHAIR.   Price $3.50.   No. 25—ROCKER.   Price $4.00.

Double woven seats and high backs.
Extreme height, 40 inches.   Seats 17 inches wide, 15 inches deep.
Weight, 17 pounds each.

One of Our Mottoes: "Prompt Shipments."

No. 26—CHAIR. Price $3.50.   No. 27—ROCKER. Price $4.00.

Extreme height, 45 inches. Seats 18 inches wide, 16 inches deep.
Weight, 24 pounds each.

No. 28—CHAIR. Price $5.00.   No. 29—ROCKER. Price $5.50.

Extra large and high backs.
Extreme height 43 inches. Seats 19 inches wide, 16 inches deep.
Weight, 25 pounds each.

Remember, All Our Chairs and Settees Are Woven by Hand.

DEN OF E. L. BOWEN, LOS ANGELES, CALIFORNIA

No. 24E—CHAIR. Price $3.50.   No. 25E—ROCKER. Price $4.00.

Extreme height, 40 inches. Seats 17 inches wide, 15 inches deep.

Weight, 17 pounds each.

They Are Worthy of Your Home and Usage.

No. 30—LIBRARY CHAIR. Price $6.00.   No. 31—LIBRARY ROCKER. Price $6.50.

Extreme height, 33 inches. Seats 16 inches wide and 15 inches deep.

Weight, 16 pounds each.

Very Light and Comfortable. Nothing Better For the Den.

No. 32—CHAIR. Price $3.50.   No. 33—ROCKER. Price $4.00.

Extreme height, 40 inches. Seats 17 inches wide and 15 inches deep.

Weight, 18 pounds each.

For Porch, Office or Club.

9

No. 26S—CHAIR.   Price $4.00.
Hickory stick seat and back.
Height over all 40 inches.
Seat 21 inches wide, 18 inches deep.
No. 27S—ROCKER TO MATCH.
Price $4.50.
Weight, 40 pounds each.

No. 35—LADY'S SEWING ROCKER.
Price $4.50.

No. 34—Chair to Match.   Price $4.00.

Extreme height 40 inches.
Seat 17 inches wide, 15 inches deep.

No. 36—CHAIR.   Price $6.00.

No. 37—ROCKER.   Price $6.50.

Extreme height, 43 inches.   Seats 19 inches wide, 16 inches deep.
Weight, 28 pounds each.

Built Especially Large and Comfortable.

No. 40—CHAIR. Price $5.50.   No. 41—ROCKER. Price $6.00.

Grandfather's Favorite.

Extreme height, 43 inches. Seats 21 inches wide, 17 inches deep.

Weight, 30 pounds each.

**The Name and Appearance Imply
Strength and Ease.**

THESE ARE THE ONES
THEY TALK ABOUT.

No. 132—CHAIR.   Price $6.50.   No. 133—ROCKER.   Price $7.00.

Height over all, 52 inches.
Seats 21 inches wide, 17 inches deep. High backs.
Catches the head just right.

Weight, 32 pounds each.

No. 36D—CHAIR. Price $6.00.   No. 37D—ROCKER. Price $6.50.

Extreme height, 45 inches. Seats 17 inches wide, 15 inches deep.
Weight, 25 pounds each.

Artistic and Very Durable.

VERANDA OF HICKORY COMFORTS, COUNTRY CLUB, LINCOLN, NEBRASKA

Massive but Not Ungainly.

No. 137—ROCKER. Price $7.50.

Wide arm rest, woven.

Extreme high back, catches the head
just right.

Height over all, 52 inches.

Seat 19 inches wide, 16 inches deep.

No. 136—Chair to Match. Price $7.00.

Weight, 32 pounds each.

Extremely Comfortable.

No. 42—CHAIR. Price $5.50.   **No. 43—ROCKER. Price $6.00.**

Extreme height, 40 inches.   Seats 17 inches wide, 15 inches deep.

Weight, 20 pounds each.

Fits the Back Perfectly.

13

Catches
the
Head
Just
Right

No. 142—CHAIR. Price $6.50.   No. 143—ROCKER. Price $7.00.

Extremely high backs. Height over all, 52 inches. Seats 19 inches wide, 16 inches deep.
Weight, 30 pounds each.

Your Order Is Not Complete Without Some of These.

No. 18D—DINING CHAIR. Price $2.50.   No. 19D—ROCKER. Price $3.00.

Extreme height, 40 inches. Seats 17 inches wide, 15 inches deep.
Weight, 15 pounds each.

A High Standard of Workmanship Is Constantly Maintained.

No. 44—DINING CHAIR. Price $3.00.   No. 45—ROCKER.   Price $3.50.

Extreme height, 40 inches. Seats 17 inches wide, 15 inches deep.

Weight, 15 pounds each.

Unequaled For Small Verandas, Cottages and Sleeping Rooms.

No. 46—DINING CHAIR. Price $2.25.   No. 47—ROCKER.   Price $2.75.

Extreme height, 40 inches. Seats 17 inches wide, 15 inches deep.

Weight, 15 pounds each.

The Only Furniture Made That Will Stand All Kinds of Weather.

15

Look for the
Green Label. The Genuine Only,
Bears Our Trade Mark.

No. 210—STOOL. Price $1.75.

Top 12 inches wide, 20 inches long,
15 inches high.
Weight, 8 pounds.

This stool goes lovely with the
Morris chair.

No. 48—MORRIS CHAIR. Price $9.00.

Extreme height, 48 inches.
Seat 22 inches wide, 23 inches deep.
Back adjustable to any angle.
Weight. 32 pounds.

**Spacious and Comfortable, Suitable
For Hospitals and Sanitariums.**

No. 140—ROMAN SEAT. Price $2.50.

Extreme height, 27 inches. Seat 22
inches long, 14 inches wide.
Weight, 14 pounds.

**No. 150—SPINDLE BACK SEAT.
Price $3.00.**

Extreme height, 30 inches. Seat 22
inches long, 14 inches deep.
Weight, 16 pounds.

RESIDENCE OF MAJOR E. W. WELLINGTON, ELLSWORTH, KANSAS,
WHO WRITES:

"I am using your Rustic Hickory Furniture on my porch the second season and like it very much. Every one of the pieces are comfortable as well as very durable. I consider it ideal porch furniture."

No. 208—FOOT STOOL.
Price $1.25.

Height 11 inches.
Top 10 inches wide.
14 inches long.

No. 220—JARDINIER STAND.
Price $2.50.

14 inches square, 29 inches high.
Suitable for Music or Magazine Rack.
Weight, 10 pounds.

No. 215—COSTUMER. Price $2.00.
Five feet high. Six hooks.
Very Convenient.
No summer cottage is complete
without a few of these.
Weight, 10 pounds.

No. 50—SETTEE, Spindle Back. Price $4.50.

Extreme height, 36 inches. Seat 36 inches long, 16 inches deep.
Weight, 32 pounds each.

Built to Meet the Demand For a Cheap Settee That Is Durable and Well Constructed.

No. 51—SETTEE, with Rockers. Price $5.00.

Same dimensions as No. 50.

No Amount of Misusage Can Impair Its Durability.

No. 52—SETTEE.   Price $6.00.

Extreme height, 36 inches.   Seat 36 inches long, 16 inches deep.
Four Cardinal Points: "Beauty, Strength,
Comfort and Price."

Weight, 34 pounds each.

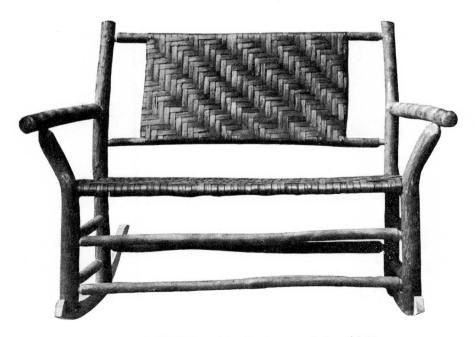

No. 53—SETTEE, with Rockers.   Price $6.50.

Same dimensions as No. 52.   Double woven seat and back.
The Only Furniture Made That Is Not Affected by Rain or Sunshine.

No. 54—SETTEE. Price $7.00.

Double panel high back.
Seat 36 inches long, 16 inches deep.   Extreme height, 43 inches.

No. 55—SETTEE, with Rockers. Price $7.50.

Same dimensions as No. 54.

Weight, 34 pounds each.

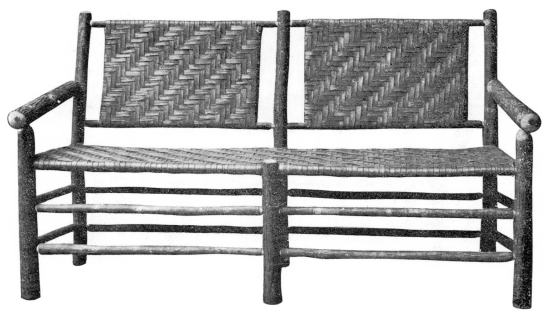

No. 56—SETTEE, Four Passenger.   Price $18.00.

Extreme height, 38 inches.   Seat 72 inches long, 18 inches deep and
18 inches high.

Weight, 57 pounds.

A Very Substantial Pattern, Well Made In Every Particular.

No. 64—SETTEE. Price $6.00.
Curved Arms.
Extreme height, 36 inches.   Seat 36 inches long and 16 inches deep.
No. 65—SETTEE, with Rockers.   Price $6.50.
Same dimensions as No. 64.
Weight, 30 pounds each.

No. 66—SETTEE, Curved Back.   Price $8.50.
Double woven throughout.
Extreme height, 36 inches.   Seat 40 inches long and 16 inches deep.
No. 67—SETTEE, with Rockers.   Price $9.00.
Same dimensions as No. 66.
Weight, 36 pounds each.
One of Our Best Values.

21

No. 70—SETTEE AND COUCH COMBINED, Double Woven.   Price $25.00.
First-class in every respect.
Extreme height, 36 inches. Seat 72 inches long, 20 inches deep and
18 inches high.
Weight, 70 pounds.

Exceedingly Beautiful.

No. 72—RUSTIC BENCH.   Price $12.00.
Height over all, 36 inches. 7½ feet long. Seat 20 inches deep.
Weight, 125 pounds.

Artistic—Durable—Comfortable.

Made of selected Hickory poles, sanded smooth.

No. 74—SETTEE.   Price $10.00.

Extreme height, 45 inches.   Seat 40 inches long, 16 inches deep.

Weight, 48 pounds each.

No. 75—ROCKER.   Price $10.50.

Same dimensions as No. 74.

These Rare Pieces Suggest Comfort and Inspire Admiration.

No. 58—COUCH. Price $16.00.

Two feet wide, 7 feet long, 18 inches high.
Light, Durable and Comfortable.
Suitable For Hospitals and Sanitariums.

Weight, 56 pounds.

**In the near future we expect the material we use to be
exhausted, but before that time comes we hope to furnish
many homes with Rustic Hickory Comforts.**

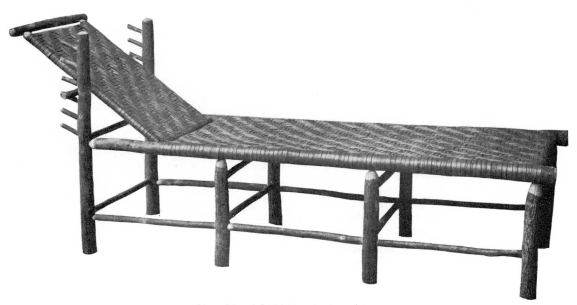

No. 62—COUCH. Price $18.00.

Frame 24 inches wide, 72 inches long, 18 inches high,
Head Rest, 20 inches wide, 31 inches long.

Adjustable to Any Angle.

Weight, 65 pounds.

24

A
TETE-A-TETE
BUILT
FOR TWO

No. 80—TETE-A-TETE. Price $8.50.

Extreme height, 36 inches. Seats 19 inches wide and 16 inches deep.

Weight, 35 pounds.

For the Summer Garden It Is Indispensable.

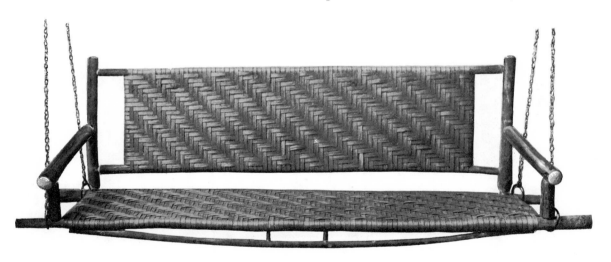

No. 96—SWING. Price $16.00.

Furnished with rings only.

Seat, 6 feet long, 20 inches deep. Height over all, 24 inches.

Four passenger.

Weight, 50 pounds.

This galvanized chain (1000 pounds tensile strength) furnished with
swings at 6 cents per foot.

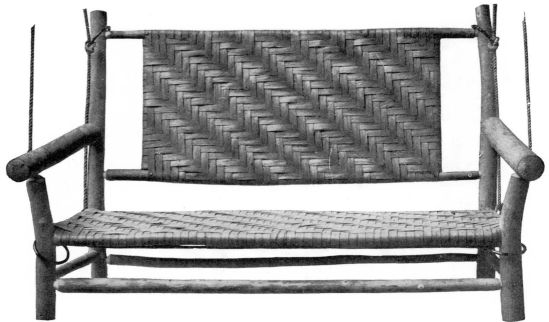

No. 90—SWING. Double Woven Seat and Back. Price $6.00.
Furnished With Rings Only.

Extreme Height, 29 inches. Seat 40 inches long and 16 inches deep.
Weight, 28 pounds.

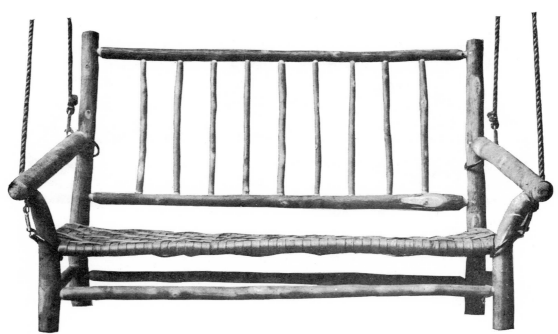

No. 92—SWING. Woven Seat.   Spindle Back. Price $5.00.
Furnished With Rings Only.

Same dimensions as No. 90.
Weight, 27 pounds.

Galvanized chain (1000 pounds tensile strength) furnished with above
swings at 6 cents per foot.

No. 99—SWING AND FRAME, with Hooks and Chains Complete.
Price $15.00.

Price of frame without swing, $9.00. Price of frame with No. 92
swing, $14.00.

The frame is fastened together with bolts and can be shipped K. D.
Height over all, eight feet.

Seat 40 inches long, 16 inches deep.

Weight, 85 to 100 pounds.

You Can Make No Mistake When You Order Some of These.

No. 97—RUSTIC SWING.   Price $10.00.

Made of selected Hickory Poles, sanded smooth.

Weight, 80 pounds.

Artistic—Durable—Comfortable.

Furnished with four chains, each 7 ft. long at $1.75 extra.

ALL OUR TABLE TOPS ARE FILLED GOLDEN OAK AND
FINISHED IN OIL, UNLESS OTHERWISE ORDERED.

No. 100—TEA TABLE.   Price $4.25.

Weight, 40 pounds.

No. 101—TEA TABLE.   Price $5.00.

With shelf 18 inches in diameter.

Weight, 45 pounds.

Round oak tops, 30 inches in diameter.   Height 28 inches.

Three Legs, Rustic.   Thoroughly Braced.

No. 102—TABLE.   Price $5.50.

Weight, 50 pounds.

No. 103—TABLE.   Price $6.50.

With shelf 21 inches in diameter.

Weight, 60 pounds.

Four Legs, Rustic.

Oak tops, 30 inches square.   Corners rounded.   Height 31 inches

No. 104—TABLE. Price $5.50.

Round oak top, 36 inches in diameter. Height 31 inches.

Weight, 53 pounds

Three Legs, Rustic. Thoroughly Braced.

No. 105—TABLE. Price $6.50.

Same dimensions as No. 104.
With shelf 25 inches in diameter.

Weight, 65 pounds.

"The furniture arriv-
ed in good time and is
very much admired."--
J. Will Johnson, Pueb-
lo, Colo.

No. 106—TABLE.   Price $6.50.

Round oak top, 36 inches in diameter.   Height 31 inches.
Four legs, rustic.

Weight, 55 pounds.

"Goods have just
been received and are
fine."—E. R. Potter,
Winnipeg, Mann., Can-
ada.

No. 107—TABLE.   Price $7.50.

Same dimensions as No. 106.   With shelf 21 inches in diameter.

Weight, 65 pounds.

Substantially Built For Summer Gardens.

30

No. 116—TABOURET. Price $1.75.

Oak top, 16 inches square.
21 inches high.
Weight, 12 pounds.

No. 118—TABOURET. Price $2.00.

Oak top, 18 inches in diameter.
21 inches high.
Weight, 13 pounds.

**No. 120—KEG TABOURET.
Price $2.50.**

Split hickory sides. Woven bark top.
18 inches high, 12 inches in diameter.
Weight, 15 pounds.
Very Ornamental.

No. 124—TABOURET. Price $2.50.

Oak, 24-inch octagon top.
Extreme height, 24 inches.
Weight, 16 pounds.

SPECIAL DESIGNS

We are prepared to build special designs of similar construction to our listed styles, and solicit the opportunity to quote prices.

———

MAIL ORDERS

Our object has always been to fill mail orders with the greatest possible speed, with the result that in most cases we have been able to make shipments the same day they are received.

We prefer to sell to dealers only, but if for any reason you can not get Rustic Hickory Furniture from your dealer, we shall be glad to supply you direct from our factory, at prices quoted herein, freight prepaid to you east of the Rocky Mountains.

———

TERMS

Dealers who are not rated by the Commercial Agencies will avoid delay by remitting with their order.

All references require from three to ten days for investigation.

To those who are satisfactorily rated, we shall be pleased to allow the regular credit terms of 60 days net cash, or less 2% for payment in 10 days from date of invoice.

Dealers remitting in advance, or buying on terms of draft against bill of lading, will be entitled to the cash discount at the same rate. All orders enclosing cash will receive our best attention.

Our responsibility ceases after goods have been receipted for in good condition by the Transportation Company.

RUSTIC HICKORY FURNITURE CO.

LA PORTE, INDIANA

32

The Wood Workers of Antiquity

Europe

Turkey

Arabia

India

RUSTIC HICKORY

A Reflection of Nature's Beauty

"Hillcrest," Summer home of Milton B. Slemmer, Centreville, Md.

RESTIN' TIME

When the blue gills are a-bitin'
An' the trout a-leapin' high;
When the bass are thick, an' fightin',
An' there's soft clouds in the sky—
Them's the times with joy a-reekin'
An' the world seems free o' care,
But when evenin' comes I'm seekin'
My old Rustic Hickory Chair.

Oh, there's lots o' joy in fishin'
When the fish are bitin' good;
An' there's lots o' fun in trampin'
With yer rifle through the wood,
But when the evenin' fire's a-glow
There's nothin' can compare
To a peaceful little hour or so
In yer Rustic Hickory chair.
—Hickory Sam.

"Welty Inn"

Du Bois, Wyoming

"Gypsy Trail Camp"

F. J. Clowes, New York City

"Beachwood Religious Association"
Undenominational chapel, Toms River, New Jersey.
A new and practical use for Rustic Hickory furniture.

RUSTIC HICKORY FURNITURE
A Reflection of Nature's Beauty

Where the ever-changing woods reach down to clear waters; where the air is sweet and the skies are smiling; where the cares of the world are forgotten and laughter is a language; where the splash of the oar chords with the whistle of the wind; where God keeps open house—there you will find Rustic Hickory Furniture.

RUSTIC HICKORY FURNITURE CO.
LAPORTE - INDIANA - U.S.A.
Nineteen Two — Nineteen Twenty-Six

1

No. 128
Table
Height 29 inches. Oak top, 24-inch octagon.

No. 616 Chair
Seat 17 inches wide, 15 inches deep, height of back from seat 21 inches.

No. 617 Rocker
Seat 17 inches wide, 15 inches deep, height of back from seat 21 inches.

No. 250 Settee
Seat 40 inches long, 16 inches deep, height of back from seat 19 inches.

No. 251—Same Settee with Rockers.

A splendid, low-priced settee. Matches the chair and rocker on this page.

An inviting settee of lasting construction.

No. 50 Settee
Seat 40 inches long, 16 inches deep, height of back from seat 18 inches.

No. 51—Same Settee with Rockers.

Seat 18 inches wide, 16 inches deep, height of back from seat 22 inches.

No. 16 Chair

Chair and rocker that will stand the hard knocks of long usage.

No. 129 Table
Height 29 inches, Oak top 25 inches in diameter.

A serviceable table for hall or porch. An ideal flower stand.

No. 17 Rocker
Seat 18 inches wide, 16 inches deep, height of back from seat 22 inches.

3

Restful as an old shoe. Rustic Hickory chairs don't need "breaking in."

Lots of room, lots of comfort, and lots of years to last.

No. 18 Chair
Seat 17 inches wide, 15 inches deep, height of back from seat 21 inches.

No. 54 Settee
Seat 40 inches long, 16 inches deep, height of back from seat 20 inches.
No. 55—Same Settee with Rockers.

No. 102 Table
Height 31 inches. Oak top 30 inches square. Golden oak finish.

Stylish enough for anywhere and big enough to be useful.

No. 19 Rocker
Seat 17 inches wide, 15 inches deep, height of back from seat 21 inches.

No. 20
Chair

Seat 18 inches wide, 16 inches deep, height of back from seat 22 inches.

A porch necessity. The children can romp on this without fear of breakage.

No. 52 Settee
Seat 40 inches long, 16 inches deep, height of back from seat 18 inches.
No. 53—Same Settee with Rockers.

A "lazy" chair and rocker with Rustic Hickory durability thrown in.

Stylish in its simplicity, with an auxiliary shelf for trinkets.

No. 103 Table
Height 31 inches. Oak top 30 inches square. Shelf 22 inches in diameter. Golden Oak finish.

No. 21 Rocker
Seat 18 inches wide, 16 inches deep, height of back from seat 22 inches.

5

Solid comfort from end to end.

No. 64 Settee
Seat 40 inches long, 16 inches deep, height of back from seat 18 inches.
No. 65—Same Settee with Rockers.

No. 22 Chair
Seat 17 inches wide, 15 inches deep, height of back from seat 20 inches.

Plenty of elbow room. An invitation to rest awhile.

No. 100 Table
Height 28 inches. Oak top 30 inches in diameter. Golden oak finish.

A fine, sturdy table, with an added touch of style.

No. 23 Rocker
Seat 17 inches wide, 15 inches deep, height of back from seat 20 inches.

Built to fit the body, and roomy enough for anyone.

Good to look at, and good to sit in. A real "cumfy" piece of ever-lasting furni-ture.

No. 80 Settee
Seat 40 inches long, 16 inches deep, height of back from seat 21 inches.

No. 36 Windsor Chair

Seat 18 inches wide, 16 inches deep, height of back from seat 22 inches.

Hickory Windsors that reflect the craftsman's skill.

Table for the reading lamp, with a shelf underneath for the photo-graph album.

No. 101 Table
Height 28 inches. Oak top 30 inches in diameter, shelf 18 inches in dia-meter. Golden oak finish.

No. 37 Windsor Rocker
Seat 18 inches wide, 16 inches deep, height of back from seat 22 inches.

7

Inside or outside, it is both useful and ornamental.

No. 82 Settee
Seat 40 inches long, 16 inches deep, height of back from seat 18 inches.
No. 83—Same Settee with Rockers.

No. 38 Chair
Seat 18 inches wide, 16 inches deep, height of back from seat 22 inches.

This chair and rocker reflect solid comfort and nature's beauty.

No. 106 Table
Height, 31 inches. Oak top 36 inches in diameter. Golden oak finish.

A fine center table for summer home or lodge.

No. 39 Rocker
Seat 18 inches wide, 16 inches deep, height of back from seat 22 inches.

8

Constructed of Nature's raw material, it fits the porch as if it were "tailor-made."

No. 90 Swing, With Chains
Seat 40 inches long, 17 inches deep, height of back from seat 19½ inches. Length over all 45 inches.

No. 40 Chair
Seat 22 inches wide, 17 inches deep, height of back from seat 24 inches.

"Grandfather's Favorite." A chair and rocker of super-comfort that have always been in great demand.

No. 107 Table
Height 31 inches. Oak top 36 inches in diameter. Shelf 22 inches in diameter Golden oak finish.

An attractive table of massive construction, with a shelf for your favorite books.

No. 41 Rocker
Seat 22 inches wide, 17 inches deep, height of back from seat 24 inches.

9

You can enjoy the evening breezes in this comfortable settee.

No. 66 Settee
Seat 40 inches long, 16 inches deep, height of back from seat 20 inches.
No. 67—Same Settee with Rockers.

Can you imagine anything more cozy than an hour or two in this chair or rocker.

No. 523 Rocker
Seat 17 inches wide, 15 inches deep, height of back from seat 20 inches.

No. 522 Chair
Seat 17 inches wide, 15 inches deep, height of back from seat 20 inches.

No. 104 Table
Height 31 inches, Oak top 36 inches in diameter. Golden oak finish.

A neat-appearing table for a dozen different uses.

10

No. 92 Swing with Chains

Seat 40 inches long, 17 inches deep, height of back from seat 19½ inches. Length over all 45 inches.

The Young folks love a porch swing, and here's one that will last for several generations.

No. 130 Chair

Seat 22 inches wide, 17 inches deep, height of back from seat 25 inches

Comfort with a capital "C." This massive Rustic Hickory chair and rocker speak for themselves.

No. 105 Table

Height 31 inches. Oak top 36 inches in diameter. Shelf 25 inches in diameter. Golden oak finish.

A dandy reading or writing table, with a big shelf for books or stationery.

No. 131 Rocker

Seat 22 inches wide, 17 inches deep, height of back from seat 25 inches.

11

Here's roominess, strength and style all in one.

No. 74 Settee
Seat 40 inches long, 16 inches deep, height of back from seat 22 inches. No. 75—Same Settee with Rockers.

High backs and roomy seats for real chair comfort.

No. 14 Chair
Seat 18 inches wide, 16 inches deep, height of back from seat 24 inches.

No. 15 Rocker
Seat 18 inches wide, 16 inches deep, height of back from seat 24 inches.

12

Take a cozy voyage on the good ship "Nature."

No. 49 Steamer Chair
Seat 46 inches long, 18 inches wide, height of back from seat 29 inches.

An unusual combination of style and comfort in this chair and rocker.

No. 26 Chair
Seat 18 inches wide, 16 inches deep, height of back from seat 29 inches.

No. 27 Rocker
Seat 18 inches wide, 16 inches deep, height of back from seat 29 inches.

Solid comfort—for a five-minute rest or an afternoon's nap. As comfortable and durable as it looks.

No. 58 Couch
Two feet wide, 6½ feet long, 20 inches high.

13

No. 76 Settee
Seat 40 inches long, 16 inches deep, height
of back from seat 20 inches.

No. 77—Same Settee with Rockers.

*Comfort from
every angle. A
pair especially
inviting.*

No. 33 Rocker
Seat 17 inches wide,
15 inches deep, height
of back from seat 20
inches.

*A splendid serv-
ing table for
summer home
or lodge.*

No. 32 Chair
Seat 17 inches wide, 15
inches deep, height of
back from seat 20 inches.

No. 112 Table
Height 30 inches. Oak
top 30 inches in diameter.
Golden oak finish.

14

Rustic Hickory products of unusual comfort, beauty and sturdiness.

No. 68 Settee
Seat 40 inches long, 16 inches deep, height of back from seat 21 inches.

No. 69—Same Settee with Rockers.

No. 42 Chair
Seat 17 inches wide, 15 inches deep, height of back from seat 22½ inches.

No. 43 Rocker
Seat 17 inches wide, 15 inches deep, height of back from seat 22½ inches.

No. 680 Tete-a-tete
Seat 36 inches long, 16 inches deep, height of back from seat 21 inches.

A chummy bit of Rustic furniture.

15

No. 94 Swing with Chains
Seat 40 inches long, 18 inches deep,
height of back from seat 22 inches,
length over all 50 inches.

*It's easy to enjoy Nature
in this comfortable swing.*

*A chair and rocker for your favorite
callers. A broad hint to stay awhile.*

No. 142 Chair
Seat 19 inches wide,
16 inches deep, height
of back from seat 29
inches.

No. 143 Rocker
Seat 19 inches wide, 16 inches
deep, height of back from seat
29 inches.

A new model—built for six. Just right for a friendly game.

No. 180 Table
Height 31 inches. Oak top 48 inches (hexagon). Golden oak finish.

These chairs and rockers will grace the finest summer homes or lodges.

No. 632 Chair
Seat 17 inches wide, 15 inches deep, height of back from seat 18 inches.

No. 633 Rocker
Seat 17 inches wide, 15 inches deep, height of back from seat 18 inches.

No. 649 Chaise Lounge
Seat 18 inches wide, 49 inches long, height of back from seat 21 inches.

Where craftsman's skill and Nature meet.

No. 46 Chair
Seat 17 inches wide, 15 inches deep, height of back from seat 21 inches.

No. 47 Rocker
Seat 17 inches wide, 15 inches deep, height of back from seat 21 inches.

Rugged and simple designs for porch or breakfast room.

No. 126 Table
Height 31 inches. Golden oak top. Open 33 x 44 inches, closed 22 x 33 inches.

A breakfast room or kitchen necessity with folding leaves for emergencies.

No. 518 Chair
Seat 17 inches wide, 15 inches deep, height of back from seat 21 inches.

No. 519 Rocker
Seat 17 inches wide, 15 inches deep, height of back from seat 21 inches.

A dining chair of style and comfort.

A comfortable rocker for the nursery.

No. 630
Chair
Seat 17 inches wide, 15 inches deep, height of back from seat 16 inches.

A lifetime comfort for the library or fireside.

No. 548
Chair
Seat 16 inches wide, 13½ inches deep, height of back from seat 17 inches.

No. 111 Table
Height 31 inches, Golden oak top 40 inches square.

A strong, good-looking table that will fit most anywhere.

No. 524 Chair
Seat 17 inches wide 15 inches deep, height of back from seat 22 inches.

A crackerjack chair for pavilion or assembly hall.

No. 525 Rocker
Seat 17 inches wide, 15 inches deep, height of back from seat 22 inches.

Mother can sew or read in comfort in these.

19

Built like the big ones. Children love their own furniture.

No. 119 Child's Table
Height 18 inches. Oak top 25 inches in diameter.

No. 12 Child's Chair

No. 13 Child's Rocker

No. 150 Child's Settee
Seat 25 inches wide.

No. 10 Child's Chair

No. 11 Child's Rocker

No. 195 Child's Swing Stand
Height over all 5 ft., width at base 4 feet.

No. 6 Child's Chair
Seat 13 inches wide, 11 inches deep, height of back from seat 13 inches.

No. 91 Swing
Seat 27 inches long, with "Y" Chains.

Strong and weatherproof. The kiddies never tire of swinging.

No. 7 Child's Rocker
Seat 13 inches wide, 11 inches deep, height of back from seat 13 inches.

20

No. 211
Stool
Height 22½ inches. Seat 12 x 13 inches.

Strong stools for many uses.

No. 210
Stool
Height 16 inches. top 12 inches wide, 20 inches long.

A rustic tabouret for the ferns.

No. 118
Tabouret — Height 22 inches. Oak top 18 inches.

No. 124
Tabouret
Height 24 inches. Oak top 24 inches Octagon.

Simple in design, with large top.

No. 116
Tabouret
Height 22 inches. Oak top 16 inches square.

No. 117 Tabouret
Height 22 inches. Oak top 16 inches square.

A rustic tabouret for many uses.

No. 140 Roman Seat
Height 27 inches, seat 22 inches long, 14 inches wide.

A bit of Roman splendor, with a touch of Nature thrown in.

21

No. 72
Settee
Seat 6 ft.
long, 18
inches
deep,
height
of back
from seat
20 inches.

No. 174 Settee
6 ft. long, 18 in. deep.

No. 70 Settee
Seat 6 feet long, 20
inches deep, height of
back from seat 19
inches.

Settees that fit everybody, everywhere. For year 'round interior or exterior use. Their cost is lost in their usefulness.

No. 93 Swing, with Chains—Seat 4½ feet long, 18 inches deep.

No. 96 Swing, with Chains.   Seat 6 feet long, 20 inches deep.

No. 97 Swing, with Chains—Seat 6 feet long, 20 inches deep, height of back from seat 21 inches, length over all 7 feet.

What is a porch without a swing? Here are some real ones.

Equally
useful
in hall
or
bedroom.

No. 265 Four Poster Bed
Inside measurements, 6 feet 4 inches long, 4
feet 6 inches wide. Head posts 5 feet high, foot
posts 4 feet high. Made any width desired.

*A massively constructed bed for lodge,
summer home or resort.*

No. 215 Costumer
Height 5 feet.

No. 260 Twin Beds
Inside measurements 6 feet 4 inches long, 3 feet 3 inches wide, head posts 50 inches
high, foot posts 40 inches high.
*Up-to-date bedroom equipment for the summer home, in typical
Rustic Hickory Construction.*

24

*Mother's favorite
for the bedroom
and porch.*

No. 45 Sewing Rocker
Seat 16 inches wide, 14 inches deep,
height of back from seat 23 inches.

No. 172 Dresser
Plain oak trimmed with Hickory. Base
20x40 inches. Mirror plate 24x30 in.

*A durable, roomy
dresser that will
appeal to every
summer home
owner.*

No. 262 Day Bed
Inside measurements,
6 feet 4 inches long,
2 feet 4 inches wide,
height over all 26½
inches.

*An inviting piece of Rustic
Hickory for that daytime nap.*

No. 114
Library Table

Height 31 inches. Oak top 30 inches wide, 60 in. long. Golden oak finish.

An attractive table for summer home or lodge, with a generous shelf underneath.

No. 240.
Folding Serving Stand— Height 30 inches, Width 20 inches.

A dining room necessity.

No. 109 Table

Height 31 inches. Oak top 30 inches wide. 60 inches long. Golden oak finish.

A splendid dining-room table of extra strong construction and generous top area.

A big, sturdy table. Plenty of room for a lawn feed.

No. 108 Table

Height 31 inches. Oak top 42x72 inches, oval. Golden oak finish.

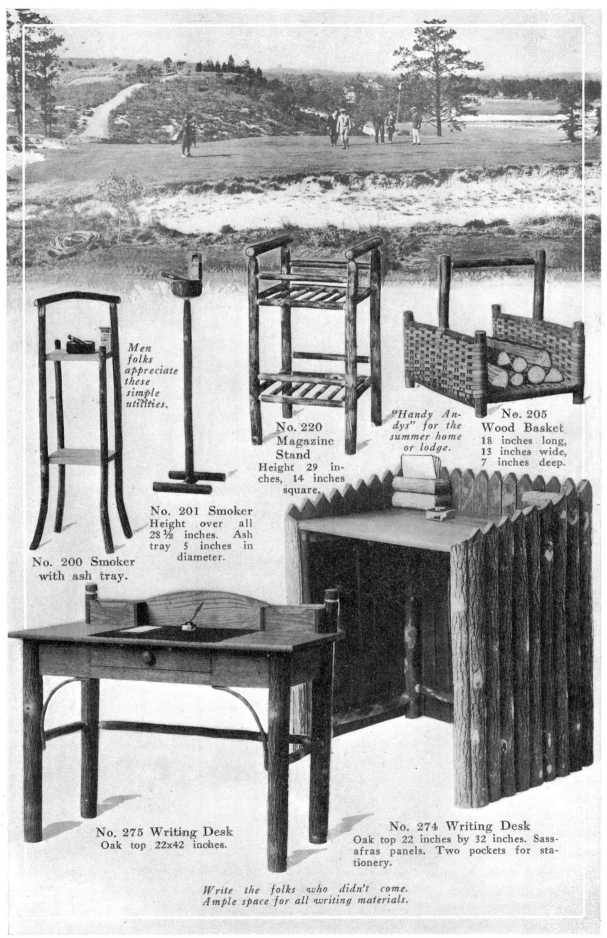

Men folks appreciate these simple utilities.

No. 220 Magazine Stand
Height 29 inches, 14 inches square.

"Handy Andys" for the summer home or lodge.

No. 205 Wood Basket
18 inches long, 13 inches wide, 7 inches deep.

No. 201 Smoker
Height over all 28½ inches. Ash tray 5 inches in diameter.

No. 200 Smoker with ash tray.

No. 275 Writing Desk
Oak top 22x42 inches.

No. 274 Writing Desk
Oak top 22 inches by 32 inches. Sassafras panels. Two pockets for stationery.

*Write the folks who didn't come.
Ample space for all writing materials.*

No. 224 Fernery
and Rose Trellis
Height over all 6
feet, width 37 inches,
removable box 9 in-
ches wide, 8 inches
deep.

No. 514 Lawn
Chair
Seat 19 inches wide,
17 ½ inches deep,
height of back from
seat 20 inches.

*A chair in
which to
dream of
woods and
waters.*

*A Rustic flower
box to grace the
lawn.*

No. 710
Rustic
Clock.
7 feet
high
over all.
Base 17
inches
by 17
inches
Standard
move-
ment.

No. 350 Lawn Settee
Seat 40 inches long, 18 inches deep,
Height of back from seat 18 inches.

*A comfortable settee that
doesn't fear the weather.*

No. 590 Tennis Seat
Height over all 26 ½ inches. Seat 51 inches
long, 19½ inches deep.

*For the player's rest between games—and
for the spectators.*

*A fine old clock for
the summer home.*

28

64

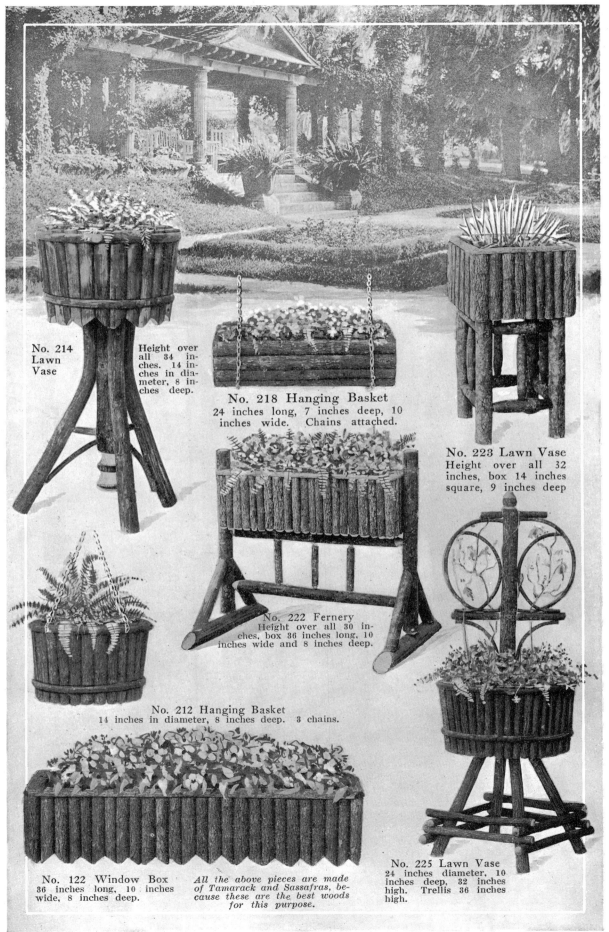

No. 214 Lawn Vase — Height over all 34 inches. 14 inches in diameter, 8 inches deep.

No. 218 Hanging Basket — 24 inches long, 7 inches deep, 10 inches wide. Chains attached.

No. 223 Lawn Vase — Height over all 32 inches, box 14 inches square, 9 inches deep

No. 222 Fernery — Height over all 30 inches, box 36 inches long, 10 inches wide and 8 inches deep.

No. 212 Hanging Basket — 14 inches in diameter, 8 inches deep. 3 chains.

No. 122 Window Box — 36 inches long, 10 inches wide, 8 inches deep.

All the above pieces are made of Tamarack and Sassafras, because these are the best woods for this purpose.

No. 225 Lawn Vase — 24 inches diameter, 10 inches deep, 32 inches high. Trellis 36 inches high.

No. 332 Rustic Tree Seat (Hexagon) 18 inches high, 5½ feet in diameter. Larger sizes quoted on request. Give diameter of tree when ordering.

A tree seat of outdoor beauty, captured for home enjoyment. Made of tamarack and sassafras.

No. 554 Rustic Lawn Chair Seat 21 in. wide, 20 in. deep, height of back from seat 22½ inches.

It radiates the beauty of the out-of-doors. Made of Tamarack and Sassafras.

No. 586 Rustic Lawn Settee Height over all 4½ feet, 5 feet long, Seat 20 inches deep. Made of tamarack and sassafras.

A stage setting for any lawn.

No. 405 Robin's Nest *A delightful sanctuary for the harbingers of spring.*

30

No. 99 Swing Stand
7 feet over all. Made any width desired.

The No. 93 Swing Seat not included.

A sturdy stand for any swing.

No. 305 Covered Lawn Seat

Height over all 7 feet, length over all 6 feet, depth 36 inches. Waterproof roof. Shipped K.D. Made of Tamarack and Sassafras.

An entrancing little rest spot for an out-of-the-way corner.

No. 420 Wren Bungalow

No. 410 Wren Bungalow

Snug little homes for the friendly birds.

No. 415 Woodpecker House
15 inches high over all.

No. 327 Rustic Summer House
(Octagon)
10 feet high over all, 10 feet in diameter. Built-in seat. Shipped K. D. flat. Made of Tamarack and Sassafras.

Vines can be trained over the roof. An ideal place for afternoon tea parties.

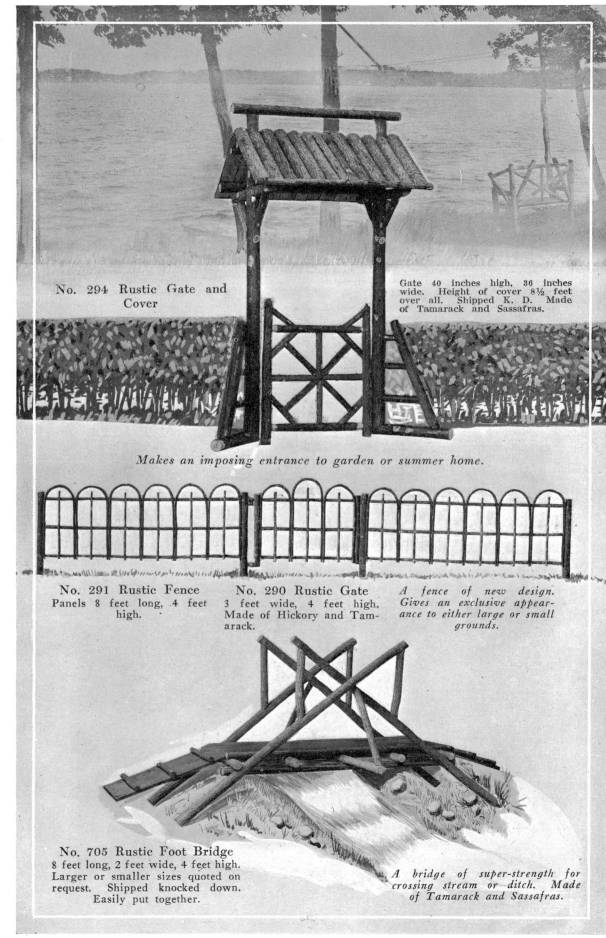

No. 294 Rustic Gate and Cover

Gate 40 inches high, 36 inches wide. Height of cover 8½ feet over all. Shipped K. D. Made of Tamarack and Sassafras.

Makes an imposing entrance to garden or summer home.

No. 291 Rustic Fence
Panels 8 feet long, 4 feet high.

No. 290 Rustic Gate
3 feet wide, 4 feet high. Made of Hickory and Tamarack.

A fence of new design. Gives an exclusive appearance to either large or small grounds.

No. 705 Rustic Foot Bridge
8 feet long, 2 feet wide, 4 feet high. Larger or smaller sizes quoted on request. Shipped knocked down. Easily put together.

A bridge of super-strength for crossing stream or ditch. Made of Tamarack and Sassafras.

32

Rest room of well-known Northern lodge, where Rustic Hickory furniture abounds.

Lobby of Yellow Banks Hotel, Webster Lake, Indiana. Rustic Hickory comfort indoors and out.

Rustic Hickory furniture around lily pond at a Summer Home near the East Coast.

Living Room of Fred W. Reed, Diamond Lake, Mich.

A Cozy Bed Room of the famous Land O' Lakes Johnson in the North Woods.

Reading room at Dune Acres Club House.

Built on one of the highest of the famous Indiana dunes. Completely equipped with Rustic Hickory furniture.

PRICE LIST
of
Rustic
Hickory Furniture

Over a quarter of a Century in the exclusive manufacture of Rustic Hickory Furniture enables us to quote you the very lowest prices possible, compatible with the highest grade of materials and workmanship.

1927

Prices Subject to Change Without Notice
All previous price lists void

RUSTIC HICKORY

LAPORTE -

PRICE LIST

Code	No.	Article	Page	Price	Code	No.	Article	Page	Price
Atom	116	Tabouret	21	3.50	*Barth*	265	Bed	24	24.00
Attest	117	Tabouret	21	4.25	*Basal*	274	Writing Desk	27	18.00
Attic	118	Tabouret	21	4.00	*Basam*	275	Desk	27	30.00
Attle	119	Child's Table	20	5.00	*Basen*	290	Gate	32	8.00
Aubin	122	Window Box	29	8.00	*Belone*	291	Fence (per ft.)	32	1.50
Auget	124	Tabouret	21	5.50	*Berlin*	294	Gate and Cover	32	45.00
Avast	126	Table	18	18.00	*Berth*	305	Lawn Seat	31	50.00
Avels	128	Table	2	8.50	*Bight*	327	House (Octagon)	31	160.00
Avid	129	Table	3	8.50	*Bigot*	332	Tree Seat	30	30.00
Avoke	130	Chair	11	16.00	*Bilbo*	350	Lawn Settee	28	10.00
Avon	131	Rocker	11	17.00	*Bilge*	405	Robin's Nest	30	2.00
Awake	140	Roman Seat	21	5.00	*Binal*	410	Wren House	31	2.50
Away	142	Chair	16	14.00	*Biped*	415	Woodpecker House	31	3.50
Awny	143	Rocker	16	15.00	*Birbo*	420	Wren House	31	3.00
Awry	150	Child's Settee	20	4.25	*Bird*	514	Lawn Chair	28	5.00
Aztec	172	Dresser	25	60.00	*Birth*	518	Chair	18	5.00
Badge	174	Settee	22	36.00	*Bland*	519	Rocker	18	6.00
Bahar	180	Table (Hexagon)	17	30.00	*Blank*	522	Chair	10	11.00
Bait	195	Child's Swing Stand	20	8.00	*Blaze*	523	Rocker	10	12.00
Baize	200	Smoker	27	4.50	*Bleak*	524	Chair	19	6.25
Baken	201	Smoker	27	2.00	*Blear*	525	Rocker	19	7.25
Balsa	205	Wood Basket	27	6.00	*Bleat*	548	Chair	19	4.00
Banco	210	Stool	21	3.50	*Bled*	554	Rustic Chair	30	12.00
Bandy	211	Stool	21	4.00	*Blend*	586	Rustic Seat	30	24.00
Banjo	212	Hanging Basket	29	5.00	*Bless*	590	Tennis Seat	28	14.00
Band	214	Lawn Vase	29	8.00	*Blest*	*595	Golf Tee Bench		18.00
Bang	215	Costumer	24	5.00	*Blet*	*596	Golf Tee Bench		22.00
Banket	218	Hanging Basket	29	4.25	*Blight*	616	Chair	2	4.00
Bard	220	Magazine Stand	27	5.00	*Blind*	617	Rocker	2	5.00
Barge	222	Fernery	29	12.00	*Blink*	*622	Chair		5.75
Baria	223	Lawn Vase	29	8.50	*Bliss*	*623	Rocker		6.75
Bark	224	Fernery	28	18.00	*Bloat*	630	Chair	19	9.00
Barm	225	Lawn Vase	29	12.00	*Block*	632	Chair	17	16.50
Barmy	240	Serving Stand	26	4.50	*Blond*	633	Rocker	17	17.50
Baron	250	Settee	2	9.50	*Blood*	649	Chaise Lounge	17	30.00
Barren	251	Rocker Settee	2	10.50	*Bloom*	680	Tete-a-Tete	15	25.00
Barry	260	Twin Beds (each)	24	18.00	*Blot*	705	Foot Bridge (per ft.)	32	3.00
Barse	262	Day Bed	25	10.00	*Blow*	710	Rustic Clock	28	50.00
		Price of Springs furnished on request.							
						*Not in Catalog			

FURNITURE COMPANY
- - INDIANA